David K. O'Hara

The Upstairs Room

Methuen Drama

Published by Methuen Drama

Methuen Drama, an imprint of Bloomsbury Publishing Plc

1 3 5 7 9 10 8 6 4 2

Methuen Drama
Bloomsbury Publishing Plc
50 Bedford Square
London WC1B 3DP
www.methuendrama.com

ISBN 978 1 472 51510 0

A CIP catalogue record for this book is available from the British Library

Available in the USA from Bloomsbury Academic & Professional, 175 Fifth
Avenue/3rd Floor, New York, NY 10010.

Typeset by Mark Heslington Ltd, Scarborough, North Yorkshire

The Upstairs Room

By

David K O'Hara

First performed in London at the King's Head Theatre
on the 13 November 2012

Cast

Gordon   Anthony Cozens
Stella   Liza Callinicos
Iris   Lucy Wray
Manager   Bret Jones

Creatives

Writer   David K O'Hara
Director   James Savin
Producers   Anthony Cozens, Steven Mills,
                        James Savin
Set Designer   Holly A Seager
Lighting Designer   Dan Saggars
Sound Designer   Max Pappenheim
Costume Designer   Ann Tutt
Stage Manager   Thom Collins
Publicist   Kevin Wilson

Anthony **Cozens** Gordon

Anthony was born and raised in Winchester. He trained at Oxford School of Drama. Acting is the only thing he's ever wanted to do, apart from a brief dalliance with wanting to be an Astronaut.

Theatre includes: *For All We Know* (Old Red Lion); *Hacked* (*Theatre* 503); *The Exonerated (*The Charing Cross Theatre); *The Common Good* (The Roundhouse studio/Arcola); *Art* (Edinburgh Fringe)

Film includes: *National Lampoons Van Wilder 2: The Rise of Taj* (MGM); *Hitler: The Origins of Evil* (CBS)

Television includes: *Sherlock;* (BBC) *Waking the Dead* (BBC); *Holby City* (BBC) *The Bill* (Talkback Thames); *Casualty* (BBC) and *Judge John Deed*. (BBC);

Anthony has also appeared in several short films including *Speechless,* winner of five awards.

Liza **Callinicos** Stella

Liza spent her childhood in South Africa and Zimbabwe, she trained in Performance at Southern Cross University (Australia), with further studies including NIDA, VCA (Aus); TVI Studios (Screen Studies – LA); Niki Flacks (UK/NYC), Martin Challis (Aus) and Zen Zen Zo (butoh/Suzuki method/ Viewpoints – Aus), RC Annie (performance combat BADC Level III – UK). She brings her unusual influences, and essential, passionate approach through the spectrum from completely natural screen roles to the most heightened and stylised physical theatre, dance and vocals.

Theatre includes: *The Enlightenment Café* (LAS theatre/Old Vic Tunnels); *Moralgorithm* (Stamp Collective/Bush Theatre); *The Screening Room Society with Robin & Partridge* (Old Vic Tunnels); *Bedtime Stories* (Edinburgh Fringe) and comedy Improv with *Laugh or Die*, alongside a fledgling Mr Brown.

Film includes: A Martial Arts champ in *Voodoo Magic* (feature – Elom Bell); Isabella in sci-fi *The Last Train* (Terry Marriott); Gabriella in *A Professional Woman* (Robin Rippman); Sonia Lane in *Love Freely But Pay For Sex* (feature – Phoenix James) and Jill in *XX/XY/X?* (Jai Young Choi, Best Short – Korean International Film Festival).

Lucy **Wray** Iris

Lucy Wray trained at the Oxford School of Drama.

Theatre includes: The Rover, *Obstacles* (New Diorama); *Swan Love* (Bush Theatre), *The Tyrannicide Brief* (Gray's Inn); *Baby Weight* (Hen & Chickens); Juliet, *Romeo & Juliet* and Viola in *Twelfth Night* (GB Tour); *Africker* (Hoxton Hall); *Rogue Taxidermy* (Waterloo East).

Along with two other actors, Lucy runs Populace, a political response theatre company. She also works with sound and performance artists, appearing at the Tate Modern and Serpentine Gallery.

Bret **Jones** Manager

Bret is a dual US/UK citizen. He works as an actor and a dancer.

Theatre includes: *WhileThe Sun Shines* (Lion and Unicorn)**;** *Cool Hand Luke* (Aldwych Theatre); *The Common Good* (Roundhouse Studio/Arcola); *Shooting Clouds* (Union Theatre); *To Kill A Mockingbird* (New Vic, Newcastle-under-Lyme); the original production of *Popcorn (*Nottingham and West Yorkshire Playhouse); the original cast of *Chitty Chitty Bang Bang* (Palladium); *Half A Sixpence (*West Yorkshire Playhouse); *Hot Shoe Shuffle (*National tour); *Shall We Dance (*European tour); *As You Like It* (Jermyn Street Theatre); *Talk To Me Like The Rain And Let Me Listen...*(Nottingham and West Yorkshire Playhouse); *My Fair Lady (*Cyprus)

Television includes: *Barrymore* (BBC); T*alking Telephone Numbers* (ITV); *Come Dancing* (BBC); *Royal Children's Variety Show* (BBC)

Films include: *Dead Thirsty* (Short); *Pride and Prejudice* (Feature)

James **Savin** Director

James studied acting at Oxford School of Speech and Drama. He used these skills in becoming a director.

Directing credits include: *Book Ends* (for The Albion Beatnick Book Store, Oxford and Summerhall, Edingburgh Fringe/The Jericho Tavern, Oxford/The One Act Festival, Lost Theatre London); *The Upstairs Room* (The Burton Taylor studio, Oxford Playhouse); *Now Until The Hour* (The Jacqueline du Pre Theatre, Oxford/The Everyman Theatre, Cheltenham) and *Finland* (The Jericho Tavern, Oxford).

James Currently resides in Oxford. *The Upstairs Room* marks his move into London Theatre directing. He is also a producer for Giddy Notion Productions.

David K **O'Hara** Writer

David K. O'Hara is a British-American playwright and novelist. He is currently based in New York.

He received his PhD in English Literature and Creative Writing at Bath Spa University in 2009. Since then, his non-fiction has been featured in various publications from *The Believer* to *Critique: Studies in Contemporary Fiction*. He most recently completed a stage adaptation of Ingmar Bergman's *The Touch*, with the blessing of the Bergman Foundation.

His work is represented by Leslie Gardner at Artellus Ltd, London.

Recent plays include: *Book Ends* (Summer Hall, 2011 Edinburgh Fringe), *Finland: A Sketch* (Jericho Tavern, Oxford), *For All We Know: A Sketch* (The Old Red Lion, RedFest, London), and *Now Until the Hour* (Cheltenham Everyman Studio).

Holly A **Seager** Set Design

Design credits include: *Hindle Wakes* (Finborough Theatre nominated for Best Designer, Off West End Awards 2012) *Chapel Street* (Underbelly at the Edinburgh Festival, winner of Old Vic New Voices Edinburgh 2012) *Clockwork Watch* (Latitude Festival); *Pandora's Box* (People Show Studio's) *Geronimo* (Company TSU at the ARC Stockton);*Tell Tales* (Bussey Building, Peckham); *They May Not Mean To But They Do* (The Lion); *Into The Woods* (Royal Conservatoire of Scotland); *Stag* (The Courtyard Theatre); *The Rising* (Gecko at the New Wolsey Theatre); *Sweeney Todd 2011* (National Youth Music Theatre at the The Rose, Kingston); *The Goodnight Bird* (Finborough Theatre). Associate Designer to Mark Friend; *Sweeney Todd 2010*, (National Youth Music Theatre, Village Underground, sight specific). Costume Supervisor to Jean-Marc Puissant; *God's Garden* (The Royal Opera House, Linbury Studio). Assistant Costume designer; *A Celebration of Young People in the Performing Arts* (National Youth Music Theatre at Buckingham Palace). Assistant Set & Costume Designer to Jason Denvir; *Who's Afraid of Virginia Woolf*,*New Boy* and *Life Coach* (Trafalgar studio's); *The Revenger's Tragedy*, (The Rose, Kingston); *All Bob's Women* (The Arts Theatre); *New Boy* (The Tabard Theatre).

Scenic art credits include: *The Veil* (National Theatre), *Castor & Pollux* (English National Opera); *Richard III* (The Old Vic) – With Capital Scenery scenic workshop.

Film credits include: *Surprise!* (Production Designer, Experimental Productions); *Waterfall on a Council Estate* (Set Dresser, Wilderness Productions).

Dan **Saggars** Lighting Design

Dan has recently graduated from Middlesex University with a BA Theatre Arts (Lighting Design and Production) and is enjoying being in the big wide world.

Design credits include: *The Story Project 3: Prayers, Promises and Platforms* at Southwark Playhouse and *The Lonely One,* a puppetry piece at the Little Angel Theatre.

Assistant Design credits include: *Romeo and Juliet* (Icarus Theatre Collective, national tour) also assisting on their touring production of *Spring Awakening* early next year, *Little Foot* (Robert Dyer, Trestle Arts Base, St. Albans) and *Phaedra's Love (*Tom White, The Arcola Theatre, Dalston). He regularly works as Lighting Design Assistant for Alex Marshall.

Upcoming projects include *The Scarlet Pimpernel* with Green Room Productions as Assistant to Miriam Evans. Dan also has extensive experience as a Production Electrician, including this year's season at Longborough Festival Opera. You can find Dan on IdeasTap (/dansaggarslighting) and follow him on Twitter (@dansaggars).

Max **Pappenheim** Sound Design

Sound Design includes: *The Fear of Breathing, Hindle Wakes, The Soft of Her Palm, Barrow Hill* (Finborough Theatre); *Kafka v Kafka, Borderland* (Brockley Jack Studio Theatre); *The Ones Who Kill Shooting Stars* (White Bear Theatre Club); *Being Tommy Cooper* (Old Red Lion Theatre); *Salome and Werther's Sorrows* (Edinburgh Festival Fringe and Etcetera Theatre). *Directing includes Perchance to Dream* (Finborough Theatre); *San Giuda* (Southwark Cathedral); *The Charmed Life* (King's Head Theatre) – Nominated for an Off West End Award 2012

Ann **Tutt** Costume Design

Ann Studied textiles at Nottingham Trent University and has previously work as a costumier.

Film credits include: *Stuart a life backwards* (Costume Supervisor, BBC); *Born Equal* (Costume Supervisor, BBC); *Straightheads* (feature); *The Pond* (Costumer designer, short); *The Knicker man* (Costumer supervisor, short) – LA Film festival winner.

TV credits Include: *Messiah IV* (Costume Supervisor); *NY-LON* (Costume Supervisor, Channel 4)

Thom **Collins** Stage Manager

Thom graduated from the Academy of Live and Recorded Arts this summer in Stage Management and Technical Theatre. In addition to the various productions, radio plays and short films that made up the two year course he has most recently been working on the 'musical comedy whodunit' *Curtains* at the Landor Theatre. He is pleased to have the opportunity to work at the King's Head for the first time.

giddy**notion** productions

Giddy Notion is a company set up to produce theatre and film that reaches a wide and eclectic audience, bringing them entertaining yet thought provoking experiences.

The company was founded by Anthony Cozens, Steven Mills and James Savin. Anthony and Steven are professional actors with twenty years' experience in the business between them and James is an accomplished theatre director who trained as an actor originally.

Giddy Notion endeavours to unite fresh new writing with a collection of bright, talented, yet undiscovered performers and creatives to develop challenging and insightful performances.

The seeds of the company were planted after a successful production of a previous draft of *The Upstairs Room*, by David K. O'Hara which sold out and garnered rave reviews in Oxford. The decision was made to take it further and build a company that could continue to create a platform for talented individuals to propel their careers and develop their craft in Theatre and Film.

Giddy – Having a reeling, light headed sensation; dizzy.

Notion – An idea, concept, or opinion

Giddy Notion productions would like to thank ...

Jim Cozens for contract advice

Alan Walsh for filming and editing film sequences

Rachel, Louisa, Holly and the staff of the King's Head Theatre

Rob at MacFarlane Chard Associates

Steven Esler for Website Design

Will Druett and the New Unity Church, Newington Green

Hanway Print Shop

The Bridge School, Islington

Pam Franklin – Artist
www.pamfranklin.co.uk

Lucy Pratt – Artist
www.lucypratt.com

OPERA &
THEATRE

Become a friend of the King's Head Theatre ...

Like our work? Want to support us? We are a completely unfunded producing house and so rely on box office sales and kind donations from members of the public that share our artistic vision and believe in what we're doing.

If you would like to make a donation and help us to continue to produce high quality work, there are a number of ways to do so . . .

Become a Friend   £25 per year

Receive our weekly *What's On* newsletter
Acknowledgment on our website

Key to the Stage Door   £150 per year

Receive our monthly friends & patrons' newsletter
Acknowledgment on our website & in programmes
Invitations to patrons' events

Key to the Dressing Room   £500 per year

Receive our monthly friends & patrons' newsletter
Acknowledgment on our website & in programmes
Invitations to patrons' events
Priority ticket booking

Key to the Theatre   £1,000 per year

Receive our monthly friends & patrons' newsletter
Acknowledgment on our website & in programmes
Priority ticket booking
Invitations to patrons' events
Free programmes for King's Head Theatre productions
Reserved seats at any performance

To discuss becoming a Friend please contact Dominic Haddock
on friends@kingsheadtheatre.com or 020 7226 8561

The Upstairs Room

Characters

Gordon, *mid-late thirties, but prematurely aged. Unshaven, crumpled, and yet handsome, tall. He wears a long overcoat and un-ironed clothes that might look respectable if they weren't so worn-out, hadn't been slept in for weeks. The impotency, the brokenness should be hidden behind an aura of frustrated power, ferocity, if not angst. That fierceness, the handsomeness in his face is a mask on the verge of breaking.*

Manager, *mid-sixties. Wears a waistcoat and a tweed blazer. Very clean cut, manicured, but masking a dissolute poverty. Rings under his eyes. A reptile. A very lonely con man who, at times, enjoys the company the con provides him.*

Stella, *late twenties/early thirties. Dark in colouring. A white blouse, black skirt, tights, worn with a long beige trench coat. A black flower is pinned to the trench lapel. Silk scarf. She is fatigued and fed-up in demeanor, but with discernible fires still smouldering within. Her seductiveness should never be overt, or too 'femme fatale'.*

Iris, *late teens/early twenties, but should be able to pass for much younger. Wears a faded tee shirt (maybe Led Zeppelin's iconic Icarus from the Seventies). Jeans, tight fitting army jacket with pockets. Slightly androgynous physically, and smaller in stature than Stella. Eager, fidgety, wild. Can be both childish and wise, almost mystic, with the abruptness and the dreaminess of a girl who's been locked away too long.*

Prologue

Low lamplight. The room is a dingy attic space, something akin to Alberto Giacometti's Paris studio. Old trunks, boxes, antiques have been piled up. Nothing older than the mid-1970s. Included in this mess, but placed more prominently are a bust of a man and an old-fashioned wireless radio. An intercom phone is mounted on the wall beside a doorway (the only point of entrance and exit). A slide projector also sits on the floor, near a dying potted fern or palm. Two couches (one green, one red) have been placed centrally, facing each other, a low coffee table between them. Stage left, there is an especially dark corner with a closet, the door of which is simply a musty curtain.

House lights fizzle out, as in a power-outage. Introductory music ends.

The room is dark now, except for the pale light falling in from a skylight.

The sound of radio static, whirring, gradually getting louder.

Iris *slips into the room through the open door, quietly, surreptitiously, with a torch. She turns on the lamps, and goes to the radio, tuning it carefully.*

A collage of interference and the sounds of the radio being tuned. Voices, screams in the night, music to appear later. Conversations to occur later. All jumbled and only vaguely discernible. Finally: Iris's song.

She switches off her torch and moves around the room, inspecting. She begins re-arranging things carefully, such as the pillows on the couches.

The movements of a girl playing, in her own private space, her own private world. We see her, at one point, acknowledge the music, closing her eyes, feeling it, mouthing the words: a favourite song.

She fiddles with the slide projector before hiding it beneath the palm tree.

Then, suddenly, she is startled by the ringing of the intercom.

She runs to the radio and switches the music off. Watches the intercom ring, waits for it to stop.

She rushes to the radio and switches it off. Then, after one last look around the room, she hurries out, closing the door very hard behind her.

Music and lights go out.

Scene One

The doorknob is rattled. Then the door gets struck from behind, with increasing force, until after a kick, it finally gives.

Enter the **Manager***, fussing with a ring of keys, followed by* **Gordon***, who holds two small cases in his hands.*

Gordon (*entering*)   It really hurts. Stings.

He stumbles a little, taking in the state of the room. He sets his bags down and comes downstage.

Manager   What's that?

Gordon   The weather. Crazy rain. Frozen in a funny way. Like shards of glass . . . almost.

Manager   Ah. I thought you were speaking . . . more generally.

He looks up.

Gordon   You been out there? The streets are a mess.

Manager   Worse things than rain I can think of.

Gordon   Sure, sure.

Manager   What with all the recent breakdowns. All these burdensome things we're now having to deal with. Bodies, for instance. Did you encounter any along your way?

Gordon   I haven't . . . No. I mean, I didn't.

Manager   No bodies? Really? They're still hurling themselves from the rooftops, I believe. Whole troupes of them, all holding hands . . . Really?

Gordon   No, no, I didn't . . .

Manager   They'll arrange to meet. In secret. Specific time, specific date. Atop one tower block or another. That's the story I've heard: complete strangers just hurling themselves over ledges. Nowhere else to go. No chance of turning back, because they've committed themselves, I suppose. Have you not encountered this? . . . My daughter says they look like lines of bunting from a distance . . . Strings of people. All holding hands, refusing to let go . . . Still holding on, even once they've . . . you know.

Gordon   No. I don't.

Manager   Can't shield your children from it enough these days: the breakdowns, the chaos that surrounds. I daresay it's made my girl a little strange. Fragile. We aren't letting her out anymore.

Gordon   So there really no windows up here?

He turns to the **Manager** *who is still looking up.*

All right. A skylight. That helps.

Manager   Yes, it does offer some relief. For me anyway, it's reminiscent of how things used to be, through there.

Gordon   A room at the top, you might say. Away from everything. The rain. Other people. I can sympathise.

Manager   Well, yes, and my wife . . . She likes to keep the lower floors to herself, empty of tenants. It's the separation.

Gordon   Yeah. The sounds of pacing feet and all that. A buffer. Don't worry. Quiet is what I'm after, what I've been longing for . . . I feel a little sick now, for some reason: all those stairs. But I suppose that's a good thing. This far up: it's further away. Much less chance of being, you know, sniffed out . . .

Manager   I can assure you, sir, we have yet to lose anyone, *anyone*. Not a single soul . . .

They both stare at each other for a moment.

Gordon   In terms of, uh, sleep, though? I don't really see –

Manager   Couches are comfortable. Most comfortable. You can't complain with couches nowadays, can you? As good as orthopaedics, these. (*He motions to the green couch.*)

Sometimes, I myself lie back rigid on this one and gaze the night away, hoping this will be the end. All over. Relief. We can finally –

Gordon (*testing the red couch*)   Okay. Yeah. This will do just fine.

Manager   Well . . . I'd suggest you sleep as little as possible. During your stay. The night especially.

Gordon (*getting up*)   Yeah . . . (*He looks around some more.*) Well, I haven't been sleeping much anyway.

Manager   Here you have . . . (*Without looking, he motions to the closet with the curtain drawn over it.*) Your facilities. Your privy chamber.

Gordon (*drawing back the curtain, and leaning his head inside*)   Spooky. Does it work?

As the **Manager** *speaks,* **Gordon** *steps inside the closet fully, opening and closing the curtain, once, then twice.*

Manager   Had it built into the old plumbings, then fit the curtain over it for discretionary purposes . . . Cleanliness, you see: it's important that you look as clean as possible otherwise, otherwise they might assume. They'll *suspect*. You have to look the part, you see.

Gordon   And to . . . ? (*He reaches out and makes a flushing motion with his hand.*) What about . . . ?

Manager (*watches Gordon, then stares up at the skylight again*)   Ah, yes, there's a system. It goes when another goes. Downstairs. Only when someone downstairs flushes do you. That's how it works.

Gordon (*from inside the closet*)   Very democratic.

Manager (*staring up*)   Keeps things inconspicuous.

Gordon (*stepping out of the closet*)   'And for my next trick, ladies and gentlemen.'

Manager   Whole room used to be storage, but obviously we've had to liquidate. The piano for instance. The chandelier. We've only a few items left. Yes, used to keep our party things up here.

Gordon   Ha.

Manager   I know. *Parties* . . . As you can imagine, we've had to make other arrangements since.

Pause.

Gordon *steps over to the shelf and stares into the eyes of the bust. His demeanor becomes fatigued, drunken.*

Gordon   Can I ask how . . . How many people have you, uh, successfully, you know . . . *spirited* away here?

Manager   Absentees, you mean?

Gordon   If . . . that's the name they're giving it now. Yeah. *Absentees*. Abstentee-*ism* –

Manager   Too many to count . . . But it's always been hotel policy, you understand, never to discuss those who come through, or those *absentees* still with us. Wife doesn't like it. The entanglements.

Gordon (*motioning to the bust*)   You probably couldn't even tell me who this numbskull is? Was, I mean . . .

The **Manager** *shakes his head.*

Pause.

Gordon   I assume my colleague Gary Hobsbaum forwarded you the necessary funds. It should cover costs. The passport, the permits, the ticket for the ferry . . . My stay. Then there's the rest of that money I'll wire you once I'm across, safe and sound. As per our agreement.

Manager   Yes . . . My wife says she has a record of the deposit. Care of Mr Hobsbaum. Ours is a system based on trust, you see.

Gordon   Yeah. Right. *Trust* . . . Old Hobs used to be based here in Hampstead, you know. Blocks away. That's where I've been while all of this shit's been going down . . . A palace of ferns and beaded curtains. 'Gord, Gord, come to England,' he tells me, this was over a year ago. 'Write your masterpiece with the best. *Trust me*,' he goes. 'Trust me . . .' Sonofabitch.

Manager *coughs.*

He's probably loving this change in the weather where he is. He got out. Before the whole country swallowed back a great big bowl of fuck for breakfast.

Gordon	**Manager** (*coughs again, more*
Hey, you know this bust?	*loudly from the word*
This bust has, believe it or	*'sonofabitch,' raising his*
not, more than just a	*voice*) Meals, sir, are
passing resemblance to	obviously included. Just
Hobs. The Hobsbaum	one a day, but it'll be
visage. He's the type of	plenty. That should keep
guy who orders himself	you going for the
wine over the telephone	duration . . . I should also
while quoting	let you know that this is
existentialist credos. A	let you know that this is
real classy sonofabitch	
. . . I'll be damned if I	
don't get at least a book	
out of this.	

Pause.

Gordon   All right. So it's starting now? Shall I just curl up in a corner and wait for you to come back?

Manager   However you wish, sir. Your papers will be arranged forthwith.

Gordon   Then it's to the south bank, and the Great Beyond.

Gordon *flicks on the radio, tuning it listlessly.*

Manager   Quite . . . For those lucky enough . . .

The radio crackles, and a clip from the Hindenberg disaster thunders out. 'It's burst into flames! Get out of the way! Get out of the way! Get this, Charlie! Get this, Charlie! It's fire and it's crashing! It's crashing terrible! Oh, my! Get out of the way, please!'

Quickly, **Gordon** *turns the radio off.*

Gordon   Sorry. (*Joining the* **Manager** *at the door.*) It's all propaganda, you know. Stock disasters to hide the present one from view. Barbed wire on the wrong side of a fence. I've heard it's useless believing any of it anymore.

Manager   Yes, well, please do try and keep the noise to a minimum, sir. For all our sakes . . . Oh and there's one last thing I must tell you, one last thing. (*Shaking his finger at the phone, beside the door.*) It's a special system we have. You must, *never* . . . use this intercom . . . Not unless you first get the signal.

Gordon   Okay . . . The signal?

Manager   Periodically, we'll ring up here with one ring – in which case you may then pick up and ring us back down in the lobby. But if this intercom rings more than once, that is, repeatedly, please do not answer. And please do not ring down. Never. It'll be an emergency. But do not ring down. We're just letting you know there is an emergency, that we have an emergency . . . within.

Gordon   And if I've got an emergency up here? If I wanna . . . talk to someone, say?

The **Manager** *just stares at him.*

Gordon   I've got to wait for you to call up . . . Aye-aye, captain.

Manager (*patting* **Gordon** *on the shoulder with the hand holding the keys*)   I'll be locking this door behind me. A precautionary measure. You'd be surprised what people are capable of, in, in . . . situations such as these.

Gordon   Better locked in here than out. I'm not going anywhere. I've got plenty of things to keep me occupied.

He mimes typing.

Manager   Next time we meet you'll be well on your way, sir . . . It looks to me like you've just about paid your dues . . . Oh, and I recommend that you be prepared to leave at any given moment. Ferry times have been very irregular as of late.

Gordon *nods.*

Manager *rattles the doorknob, then departs, slamming the door behind him. The sound of locks being turned.*

Gordon *turns around, taking in the room as if for the first time, looking genuinely afraid. Then he faces the bust again.*

Gordon (*sighing*)   Sonofabitch.

He goes to the smaller of the two cases he brought in and opens it. Very carefully, he pulls out a typewriter and sets it on the low coffee table between the two couches. He coughs, pulls his coat tight around him.

Gordon   Okay. So, this is what you wanted. A perfect bubble of suspense. No more distractions. All that booze in Hobsbaum's medicine chest. Pornography. Time to dry out but not up. No more persecutions or screams in the alleyways. No more obligations . . . Everything's still raw, so c'mon. Let's go. You're as good as dead now too. (*Realising.*) And . . . without . . . any . . . paper. Jesus.

He quickly paces around the room, searching. He notices a slide projector lying upside down beneath one of the plants, and he sets it right. He takes up the cord with the small remote on the end of it.

He flicks the switch a number of times.

Gordon   No. Distraction. I need – I was looking for . . .

He sets the cord down again and flips the projector over, the way it was lying before.

Gordon (*again surveying*)   My kingdom . . . My kingdom for
a blank sheet of . . . *C'mon*.

*He furiously turns over the cushions on both couches and, inside the
red one, finds a book, a thick paperback.*

Gordon (*reads aloud*)   'The Phenom-en-ology of Perception.'
You must be joking me. (*Leafing through the pages for a moment,
then weighing the book in his hands*.) *Heartbreaking* stuff.

*He holds the book out towards the typewriter and seems to imagine a
way of feeding it into the machine. Then he tosses it back onto the
couch. He fakes a laugh as he steps past the eye line of the bust. He
stands there, defeated.*

Gordon (*up at the skylight*)   Paper?

*He rushes over to the intercom, reaches out, then stops himself. An
idea is dawning on him.*

Gordon   'Man's lot in the universe . . . Clinging . . . clinging
to . . .' Not now. Wait. Just wait. Six months of nothing, and
now this.

*He runs to the closet and tests the material of the curtain. He looks
back at the typewriter.*

Gordon (*realising, throwing open the curtain*)   No. no. Wait just
a sec.

*He steps fully into the closet, roots around inside. A long pause
follows before he jumps out, holding three rolls of toilet paper in his
arms.*

Gordon   Ta-da.

*He rushes quickly over to the typewriter and proceeds to feed one of
the toilet paper rolls into it.*

Gordon (*bad French*)   *Les mierdes des les artistes*. (*Locking down
the paper, putting his hands on the keys*.) Okay. Man. Always
clinging. (*He begins to type.*) 'Man's tendency to cling
desperately to others, even though he always ends up . . .
sinking in the process . . .' Man then glares at the page, sees if

he can make out text on single-ply. 'The writing on the roll
. . .' Wait, is that: *stinking*? Did he really go and write
'stinking,' here? Nevermind. Continue. *Gordon*.

*He types furiously for a few moments. In elongating spurts. Then,
after one, last, lingering, pause, he hits a single key. Then he
carefully rolls the paper back up to read.*

Gordon   All right. So, what've we got . . . 'Man's tendency'.
Blah-dee-blah. Sinking, not stinking. Okay . . .' The truth.
Yes, the truth of writing functions as a life raft.' Life-*preserver*,
I should have said. 'Truth means liberation. Fighting for
absolute clarity and . . . facticity. Lifting us up from the icy
depths. All that suffocating fear and darkness.' A little cliche,
but . . . I like it. I like it. Hobsbaum'd eat this shit up. He
loves big ideas. But what's all this? 'The little bridge?' No . . .
'You and I? Lying back in the long grass . . . the sunlight . . .
The wind . . . trees blowing . . . and the little bridge . . .' No.
'Broken glass?' No. That's really too much.

*He stands up, contemplating. He shakes his head. He looks down at
the projector, stares at it, realises he's staring at it, then shakes his
head. He steps casually over to the second case he brought in, places
it on the couch.*

Gordon (*releasing one latch*)   Dis. (*Releasing the next latch.*)
Tract. (*Lifting the lid.*) *Shun.*

*After one or two items of loose clothing and some magazines, he lifts
a false beard out of the suitcase. It should be laughably bad. A little
goatee in two pieces, to match the beard on the bust.*

Gordon   A mirror. Have-you-gotta-have mirrors for this?
. . . Really? . . . Maybe just a window pane. No? Or a shard of
. . . Neither paper nor reflections . . . Really nothing? . . . A
room, a situation, sans reflection . . . He will have to trust
himself. Alone. And not for the first time. (*Placing the beard
carefully on his face.*) Man alone in the universe, must manage
. . . his own disguises. Guard his own otherness above all
others. (*Coughs, putting on an English accent.*) 'My name, now
my name, ladies and gendarmes is Lord Gary. That's

Hobsbaum, ladies . . . May I please have an order of 12 *Sangiovesy*, 24 Merlot, oh and one passport for my good man, Gordo, too. Yes, perhaps a deus ex machina to dangle down, mercifully, to him in this shameful self-predicament of his, underlining, absolutely, above all, that hell is without a doubt . . .' What-was-it-again? . . . yeah, 'other people . . .' (*With disgust.*) Blah . . . This glue. It's too much.

He tears off the beard, as if revealing himself dramatically, defiantly, to the bust. Then he slumps down on the green couch.

Gordon (*with growing vehemence*)   No . . . No. It's all distractions. And still: no paper. Goddamnit. Look. (*He stands.*) Here I am. Maskless. Do you see me? Huh? Can't you? (*He jumps onto the coffee table, his legs either side of the typewriter, and screams to the skylight.*) Look at me. I'm still here. Look, now: I'm still here you sons-a-bitches.

Black.

Scene Two

Lights rise, slowly, to a bare minimum of visibility.

The green couch has now been overturned, the typewriter just visible on the floor in front of its foremost point.

The projector now sits on the coffee table where the typewriter used to be. It is now running, casting a blank square of light around the doorway.

The three rolls of toilet paper have been unravelled in different directions.

The door is suddenly kicked. Long pause.

The door is kicked twice, the knob rattles. Sounds of locks being turned.

Gordon (*dazed, from underneath the couch*)   Jes-us.

One more kick and the door finally gives.

Manager *enters, propping up the half-conscious* **Stella** *whose arm is draped over his shoulder. He's momentarily blinded by the projector-light.*

Manager (*anxious*)   Hello? Hello, sir? (*To himself, gasping.*) What's his name? (*Shouting.*) *Sir.* It's time. You must . . .

Gordon *gives an almost frightened-sounding groan from beneath the couch.*

Manager, *rushes, stumbling, leading* **Stella** *into the closet. (She is missing a shoe.) He manages to get her in first, then follows from behind, closing the curtain. A light goes on inside.* **Stella** *groans, seems to be formulating the word 'no'.* **Manager** *groans. There is the sound of a tap running for a moment, then a pause. Then the sound of* **Stella** *choking, or throwing up.*

Gordon *worms his way downstage, head-first, out from underneath the couch. On his face, he wears the false moustache.*

Gordon (*pushing the typewriter out of his way*)   I'm having . . . (*Announcement.*) I think I'm having an attack, here. Of some kind.

Light goes off in the closet and the **Manager** *leaps out, again stumbling, tucking in his shirt-tails.*

Manager   It's time, sir.

Gordon   Hello?

He feels along the wall and switches on the floor lamps – as **Gordon** *simultaneously proceeds to crawl over to the coffee table and turn off the projector by swatting it repeatedly.*

Manager   The ferry. Didn't you hear us ringing? Earlier? It's time, it's time. Your papers –

Gordon (*out of breath, holding onto the overturned couch like a life-boat*)   How long? You said forthwith. You told me: trust. And you left me here . . . Without anything.

Manager   Sir. I assure you it's been little more than twenty four hours. Really. A single night.

Gordon (*standing up, brushing himself down*)   Five days. Five days. That's light, dark, light, dark, light. I counted. Five times over. Back and forth.

Manager *begins collecting* **Gordon**'s *clothes off the floor and throwing them into the typewriter case.*

Manager   I think you're very much mistaken. Now if you please . . .

Gordon   But. No. How could . . . How long, did you say? No way. No.

Manager   How many meals do you remember? Precisely. There was the potato dauphinoise I delivered last night, on a bed of rocket, coffee in the morning. And?

Gordon   The dauphinoise . . . The thermos of coffee.

Manager   Yes? What else?

Gordon   And, uh . . . It was all coffee and potatoes. Wasn't it?

Manager *yanks a little manila envelope out of his pocket.*

Manager (*furiously tidying*)   Your papers, sir. Professionally fabricated in record, I assure you, record time. Your being American helped. There are still some strings to be pulled at what's left of the embassy. Your name is still the same but you're married now, living in sunny Pennsylvania with an English wife who gives you a hard time. You also have a daughter who's a history of schizophrenia and who's just gotten herself committed. That's why you're going back, that's why you're getting out. Motive, you see. I thought of it myself: no one can deny you such obligations, can they? Anyway, you've been made a foreign correspondent now too, a real writer. Your job here is done.

Gordon (*confused, taking the envelope*)   I am a real writer. An all-rounder. I've been working on a book. Freelance –

Manager (*from 'all rounder'*)   Then splendid, splendid. It's all worked out very well, hasn't it? Now, if you please. Sir.

Manager *begins uprighting the couch, and* **Gordon** *helps him.*

Gordon (*helping, straining himself*)   Six months now, I've been cracking away at it. I don't have anything yet, per se. But I've got pages. Plenty enough for a rough draft. At least.

As soon as they have finished, they both collect **Gordon***'s things and pack them away, clothes inside the typewriter case, typewriter inside the suitcase.*

Gordon   This is real provocative stuff. Which means I've got to keep most of it upstairs, at the moment, locked in my head, you know?

Gordon *dazed, follows the landlord to the door, his things in his arms.*

Manager (*pulling* **Gordon** *from the room*)   You know your way then, do you? Straight along, right down the embankment. You're bound . . . Bound to meet the proper authorities. Look for the uniforms. At the first checkpoint, present them with your papers . . . And don't forget the, um, disguise we recommended.

On the word 'disguise' **Stella** *stumbles from the closet and both men watch hypnotised as she moves over to the green couch and collapses.*

Manager (*watching*)   And . . . your papers, yes, in the . . . I just gave them . . . yes . . . You can just about make it now, if you . . . Here we are.

Gordon   Is she? . . . What's happened to her?

Manager   Who? Yes, well, the underground got to her, didn't it. It's always the underground inevitably. Interrogated. Drugged, I'm sure. Taken hostage. Maybe even . . . If I've seen it once if I've seen it hundreds of times. All the more reason . . . So now, if you please . . . *Please.*

Gordon   But . . . why's she here? I mean, why have you brought her all the way up here?

Manager   Precautionary. You see, we're depended upon. For the particular services we can provide here. The poor dear needed spiriting away, and she came to us seeking a little guidance. A little sanctuary. And I thought, as you were on your way out . . .

Gordon   So she's . . . like me? An absentee or whatever you call it?

Manager   No . . . *Yes*, indeed, she's –

The intercom phone rings twice. Then silence.

Gordon   Does this count as one ring or two?

Pause.

The phone rings again.

Manager   No, it'll be my wife. My wife. No, she thinks I'm still . . . Blast. It's probably my daughter, once again, wreaking havoc.

He scrambles to find his keys as the phone continues to ring.

Long pause. Ringing ceases.

Gordon   I'll stay.

Manager   You'll what?

Gordon   I'm gonna stay . . . Look after her. She looks like she –

Manager   Here? I don't know. Are you certain you can?

Gordon   Yeah.

Manager   After all this time alone, I don't think you're in any state to tackle . . . to *handle* –

Gordon (*putting his things down*)   Look, I'll make sure she doesn't try anything crazy. Doesn't start screaming the whole building down because someone's gone and locked her in an upstairs room with . . . just a skylight for company.

Phone rings again. This time rapid-fire, impatient.

Manager   Are you very sure about this? No, because. This is highly irregular. No one's ever . . . once they've received their papers. Are you absolutely . . . ?

Gordon *nods.*

Phone rings.

Manager *peers over at* **Stella** *and nods. Then he gives* **Gordon** *a territorial squint.*

The **Manager** *steps out, leaving the door cracked ajar. Meanwhile,* **Gordon** *lifts the phone, so that it stops ringing. He holds it in mid-air for a few seconds, then sets it back very carefully beside the door.*

He steps behind the curtain and we hear him washing his face. The toilet flushes. He comes back out a few moments later with a glass of water in his hand. The moustache is gone. He crosses the room, carrying the glass extremely carefully, to stand before the coffee table.

Gordon (*whispering*)   Underground, huh?

He sets the glass of water down on the coffee table, then moves the glass nearer to **Stella**'s *side. He scoots the coffee table closer to her too. Then he stands over her, recognises that she is asleep. She re-adjusts herself, turning towards him but now on her side. He removes his coat and puts it over her.*

Unsure what to do with himself at this point, he leans back on the opposite couch, and looks up at the skylight.

The lamplight flickers. Fades. Black.

The projector goes on. Then a number of blank slides go flicking by.

Suddenly, we come to images of **Gordon** *running through a wooded area, as if being chased. He is wearing a moustache, perhaps a real one this time.*

In the very last shot (no longer static), we see him catching his breath, smiling as he looks up, then embracing the woman who has been waiting for him. We don't see her face. Only his face nuzzling the side of her neck.

Blank projector light.

Scene Three

The lights rise. **Gordon** *switches the projector off.*

Gordon   It's coming back.

Stella (*raising a hand*)   Just stay where you are, for just a minute, would you? I can't –

Gordon   No, it's okay, it's okay. How are you doing?

Stella   How long have I? . . . I didn't . . . ?

Gordon   No. I dunno. Sounded to me like they just dragged you in off the street. Is there a story there?

Stella   What time is it?

Gordon   Early morning, I think.

Stella (*looking up at the skylight*)   Early morning?

Gordon   What's the last thing you remember?

Stella   The very last thing? I remember . . . Sleep. What's the last thing I *want* to remember would probably be a better question . . . though the answer would be, now that I think about it, very much the same. One . . . long . . . sleep.

Gordon   In one of the stations, maybe? Is that where you've . . . been . . . ?

Stella (*sitting up, upon her elbows*)   No . . . (*She glares at* **Gordon**, *taking him in*.) What do I look like to you?

Gordon   Well, you're missing your, uh . . . You –

Stella   I live in Hampstead.

Gordon   No, the manager here, the seedy little guy who runs this operation, he mentioned . . . you'd been . . . something had happened to you on the underground.

Pause.

Stella   Oh. I see. Yes: underground . . . I'm afraid you may have confused the 'whom' with the 'where.'

Beat.

Gordon   Oh, I get you. It's *an* underground. People you mean, who make up an underground.

Stella   Yes, as opposed to *the* . . . Anyway, it's just a story. Something I fabricated for the hotelier so that he'd let me in out of that rain . . . I think I must have fainted after. I didn't, you see, I didn't want to die out there alone on the street. (*Suddenly on the point of tears*.) In all that horrid weather. Just another body . . . I thought I was dying, actually . . . And I panicked . . . I might be dead now, for all I know. This place could just be my whole dismal life flashing before my eyes . . . An empty room, a skylight. (*Laughs*.) Serves me right.

Gordon (*reassuring*)   Hey . . . Hey, maybe we should . . . Let's try something else, okay? What about this underground? Could you, maybe, tell me about them, who they are, what they want?

Stella   Well, they're an underground, aren't they. So, that presupposes a certain level of obscurity.

Gordon   I see.

Stella   No you don't. Nobody does. It's all just groping in the dark.

Stella *sits up, throwing the coat off, and begins gulping back the glass of water.*

Gordon   Yeah. Well, okay. Maybe I can . . .

She continues to drink, holding her hand up to silence him. Pause.

Gordon   You don't want me to tell you where you are, at least?

Stella (*finishing the water*)   What? No. Not really. No.

She leans back on the couch with relief. Long pause.

Gordon   It's a holding place, sort of. A stop gap, for those of us seeking a way out. If we make the right connections, see, we can escape. We can just go. There are still ways to leave. And this, well this is just the last stop. Before we get spirited away. Like a, what-do-you-call-it? Ellipsis. Dot dot dot.

Stella   Oh, one of those.

Gordon   Yes.

Stella   And is that what you're doing here, then – dot dot dot?

Gordon   I guess so. Avoiding the tyranny of the period (*laughs*) . . . I mean the, uh, full-stop.

Stella   Oh, American . . . So you're . . . Ha, well, this is funny. I'm sorry. I didn't quite . . . You know, you're probably one of the very last.

Gordon   I guess I arrived just as they were all jumping ship, rushing back across the pond. It was quite freeing, you know . . . to be heading the other way. Cutting through this wave of people. Everyone: Americans, Brits trying to get to Florida, just staring at me dumbfounded with their bags.

Stella   In that case . . .

She stands wearily, finding her feet, awkwardly because of her shoe. She motions to **Gordon** *with both her hands.*

Stella   Could you come? Over here.

He stands, slowly leaning towards her across the coffee table, but before he can touch her, she slaps hard him across the face.

He lowers himself back onto the couch. He puts his head down for a moment, seems to spit something into the armrest.

Gordon (*looking up*)   What was that?

Stella (*now leaning back on the couch*)   For queen and country.

Gordon   What?

Stella   Don't be daft, it's just an expression. To differentiate us from you lot.

Gordon   Okay. But why . . . ?

Stella   Because you let this happen. If you hadn't sat on your bloody hands when everything started . . .

Pause.

Gordon (*massaging his jaw*)   Not me personally. Did you really – ?

Stella   You didn't stop me . . . And what about you? You, specifically. What kind of masochist comes here . . . to this? You must be a real egomaniac. Either that or just unbelievably idiotic.

Gordon   Sure, okay, I kinda . . . put my finger on a map and booked the ticket. But I thought I needed . . . to . . . uh . . . I don't know.

Stella (*laughs*)   What? . . . You needed? . . . What did you need?

Gordon   No. No. I don't know. I needed . . . New material.

Stella   Well there's plenty of that here, mister. Falling from the sky, primarily, in little grey flakes. Everywhere, ambiguous matter. Bits of brain. Bits of skin.

Gordon   Okay. Stop it.

Stella   Well, you never know.

Pause.

Gordon   When I first got here, I kept wondering why they had to hose down the city every night. The sound of all that water, rushing, hitting the streets with a slap, just outside the windows. Flopping like a dead fish. For the longest time, I thought it was all just part of the weather. The fall-out. But every night, dead on time: *whoosh* . . . Then. (*Laughs.*) I got it in my head that this was the sound of everything sinking, a whole sinking country. You're an island after all. And I heard it deflating out there, very slowly. I had to hit the typewriter keys extra hard to keep my mind off the thought. All that sinking.

Stella   So you're a *writer* then, are you? (*Holding her arms out once more, motioning to him.*) Well, why didn't you say? . . . Shall we try this once more, or have you had enough?

Gordon *shakes his head. He just leans forward, elbows on his knees.*

Gordon   C'mon.

Stella   No? . . . Perhaps you're just a typist.

Gordon   Look, what've you got against writers? Against me?

Stella   Nothing. My father was one of your ilk, in fact . . . You're all egomaniacs, aren't you? Yes, it's part of the profile. A prerequisite. Men in their offices. He had this little artisan's moustache, just like the one you see over here. (*Directed towards the bust.*) Handsome. My handsome, moustachioed father. With a knack for the idiotic, rather like your own.

Pause.

Gordon   You done?

She shrugs. Pause.

Can't you see I'm trying here?

Stella (*laughs*)   Trying? Trying what exactly?

Gordon   I just thought, maybe I could help. Maybe we could help each other out, okay? Since we've both ended up here, in the same place. *Of all the places.* The management, you know – if it weren't for me, you'd probably be doing Faye-Dunaway-tied-to-the-john-in-that-Robert-Redford-movie right now. All right? (*Carefully, he reapplies the moustache.*) Let's start over: the name's Gordon. I'm . . . American. And I apologise for everything. Okay? Your turn.

Pause.

Stella   So you're playing Robert Redford now?

Gordon   I'm playing Robert Redford playing me.

Beat.

Stella   All right. So, how does this go? My name is Stella . . . my country you've . . . already been acquainted with . . . And I regret nothing . . . Okay? Gordon?

Gordon   Okay. So tell me, then. I dare you. Chapter One, Stella. How does this regret-free story begin?

Stella   With being born. Birth I suppose you'd call it. Just like everyone else.

Gordon   Mm-hm. And you have no regrets about that . . .

Stella   None. Mother welcomed me into this world crouched on all-fours. Rather than lying back, because that was never her style. My Great Unsinkable Mummy. Father, meanwhile, was a mediocre photographer who taught photography. At a special school down the road. I was his favourite model for a time, and mummy never forgave him for it . . .

Gordon Wait, I thought you said writer.	**Stella** Would you like to know about the time I saw them fucking?

Beat.

Gordon   You said your father was a writer.

Stella   No, I said he was one of your ilk. I suppose that was because you have similarly interrogative bedside manners. I was reminded. Or was it your obliviousness? I don't know. No, I'm sorry, he taught photography to the mentally ill, schizophrenics . . . retards . . .

Pause.

Gordon   Continue?

Stella   With the fucking?

Gordon   No, 'cos I don't buy that. It's the cliche of cliches.

Stella   A cliche from which we all spawned.

Gordon   Yes. Well. Give me something more, you know, original.

Stella   Something else?

Gordon   Sans regret.

Stella   Sans? . . . Well, let me see. This is going a long way back, isn't it . . . but all right. We lived in palatial house until I was fourteen, fifteen.

Gordon   Mm-hm.

Stella   A lovely place, but very very dark. Thick with ivy. Windows all cast in shadow, shaded. Very cool and calm in the summer. Floors of bare wood. I doubt it exists anymore. It had this long gravel drive, I remember. And a rock pool. And then there was this mysterious upstairs room I discovered one day and turned into my own.

Gordon   Yes?

Stella   It was a frightening place, really. Cobwebbed, dusty. But I used to . . . well, I used to hide up there.

Pause.

Gordon   From what?

Stella   From everything . . . Well, no, nothing, really. Just stupid things that make a girl cry. Cliches of the heart. Anyway, daddy was preoccupied with his dark room pictures and mummy was always too busy with her martyrdom, so I used to climb up there, to the upstairs room of our house, and very carefully I would lock myself inside. I think it had once been a storage space of some kind, or a nursery. Like a small attic. Very low roof. Skylight . . . I used to write letters up there, you know, until it was quite late. Pouring my heart out. No one ever came looking for me, funnily enough. I was too careful.

Gordon   Tell me about the letters.

Stella   Yes, I wanted to write poetry, you know. Daydream, draw pictures . . . but I felt, I always felt, I should be sending these to someone. Even the most intimate of intimate details I had to make believe I was sharing with *somebody*: imaginary sisters, imaginary men. All of them living in faraway locales. Imaginary cities. It was thrilling for me, thinking of all these, all these other people, these shadowy recipients, you see. That, I suppose, was the real point of it: their hands slowly unfolding the envelope, their eyes moving over my words. It was almost licentious. Poetic licentiousness, you might call it. Afterwards, I would stuff these letters away in the floorboards, folding them up, again and again, until they were invisible, out of sight.

Gordon   Sans regret?

Stella   No. Sans nothing. It was a protective urge. A carefulness on my part.

Gordon   What happened to them? Do you know? Those people, those letters?

Stella   Time went by, and I forgot them, I forgot all the time I'd spent in that room . . . Then, as fate would have it: (*Beat.*) a Croatian family moved in next door to us, with this beautiful boy named Dragan. And this Dragan and I, we decided we should have ourselves a secret place to talk and smoke cigarettes. So I led him by the sleeve one afternoon, up to this dusty old upstairs room I hadn't visited in years. With the low roof, the skylight. It was scarier than before, I remember. There seemed to be another presence, like someone, or something, hiding up there with us . . . Everything was starting then, the snows were already coming and the transports were in full swing, and there was just the two of us, me and this boy named Dragan, talking and smoking and fooling around. It was then, I think, I lost my sense of carefulness. (*Pause.*) I suggested we go round the room and *pluck* all my old letters out of their hiding places.

Gordon   You read them?

Stella   No.

Gordon   Then what? Stella? What did – ?

Stella   Burned them. Made a little bonfire. Dragan didn't want to, said I would burn the house down, that we'd be caught, but I did it anyway. The whole lot. You see, the last thing I wanted was to remember what I'd written, hidden so bloody bloody carefully all those years ago. We got ashes everywhere, literally everywhere, in our hair, on our skin . . . Naked, rolling around . . . Careless.

The lights flicker.

Gordon   It's going again.

Stella   It's been going for months. Haven't you noticed? And yet, here we sit, talking like this, like nothing's happening.

Gordon   It'll be light again soon. If it's early morning. We can continue. We should.

Long pause.

Stella   No, I think it's past. I think you have the time all wrong, Gordon. Just like me . . .

She reaches for the projector, just as the lights begin to flicker again.

What's on this?

Gordon   Nothing. There weren't any slides in it the last time I looked.

Lights flicker out, and **Stella** *switches on the projector.*

She begins flicking through the empty slides, just as **Gordon** *did earlier.*

Suddenly: still images of **Stella** *and* **Gordon** *in bed together. Breakfast trays, newspapers. Morning light. Final image is of* **Stella** *lighting* **Gordon***'s newspaper on fire, laughing. Movement: they kiss.*

Black.

Scene Four

Sound of rain.

The phone rings, once.

Blank light of the projector cast on the wall. The red couch has been overturned.

Stella *is straddled over* **Gordon***, whose legs stick out from behind the couch. What seems to be a struggle between the two of them turns out to be sex. There has been a minimum of disrobing.*

Stella   Don't come, okay? (*She pounds her fist on his chest.*) Don't come just yet.

Gordon   Okay. Inside you, or?

The phone rings once: the signal.

Stella   Move. Here.

They change position.

Gordon (*breathless*)   Okay. Wait.

Stella   Stop talking.

The phone now rings repeatedly.

Gordon   There's something wrong. That's the –

Stella   Stop. Don't. Stay, just there.

Gordon   Wait.

Stella   No. I said. Keep . . . Yes, right.

Gordon   Okay. Oh my God. Oh my God, I love you.

Ringing stops.

Stella   Mother. Fuck. Yes.

Gordon   You're so fucking . . . Hang on, hang on, hang on. Oh my God.

Just as he slows, just as the sound of their breathing really synchronizes, **Iris** *steps carefully into the room. She watches the couple for a moment, then checks behind the door. Carefully, she closes the door behind her.*

Gordon *and* **Stella** *resume, more aggressively.*

Stella   Yes. Yes. Yes, fucking. *Yes.*

Standing in the projector's light, **Iris** *pulls out a torch and raises it in their direction. Holds it.*

Stella   You're going . . . .You're going to kill me. You. Mother . . . Ffff.

Gordon   Oh, Jesus, tell me. You love me. Tell me . . .

Stella   Wait.

Iris *lowers the torch. She turns away and looks around the room for a place to hide.*

Gordon   Sorry. Sorry. I just.

Stella   No, it's not right. This doesn't feel right.

The phone begins to ring, sporadically. Last gasps.

Noticing the curtain, **Iris** *rushes as quietly as possible over to it. She slips behind the curtain and hides.*

Stella (*sitting up*)   I can't.

Gordon   But. No. You were almost . . .

Long pause.

Stella (*feeling around the floor for a missing stocking*)   I can't.
No.

Gordon   But this is okay? Isn't it? Just come here. Let
me . . .

He places a hand on her shoulder.

Stella   What am I doing? What are you . . . What do you
think you're doing?

Shrugging his hand away, she shakes her head no.

Gordon   Hang on a second. What just . . . ? You don't just
. . . *change* like that.

She stands up, pulling her tights back on.

Stella   Well, I do . . . I can.

She rushes over to turn on the lights as **Gordon** *lays back down
beside the overturned couch. The lights go on just in time to show
him zipping himself up. Then* **Stella** *goes over to the coffee table and
slams her palm down hard on the projector until it switches off.*

Stella   Don't be such a little girl, Gordon. These things
happen. There's no need to sit here and sulk.

Gordon   These things happen? Didn't you hear the
intercom? That, there, was an emergency. That's what it
means, you know. And we missed it.

Stella   I really don't see what bloody difference it makes.
We're in a terminal state of emergency.

Gordon *sits up, just as* **Stella** *sits down on the green couch hugging
her knees. He then uprights the red couch.*

Gordon (*straining*)   The point is, honey, that there is an
emergency within. The barbarians are at the gate. There's

probably a whole mob of them, right now, downstairs, dressed in black, searching this whole building. Sniffing out impostors, absentees . . .

Stella   Oh God. That old story. What does it matter, one way or another?

Gordon   They're out for vengeance, Stella.

Stella   What for?

Gordon   Well . . . for *everything*. I don't know: all of this. Someone's gotta take the blame. And they're bound to find us. Of course they'll find us. The buck stops here. At best, you're gonna be back out on the streets again, alone . . . Or, worst case scenario: you and I both get cuffed and rubber-gloved and taken down for questioning, and that's before they decide whether or not to send us off to God knows where. C'mon, you-tell-me: where is it they send people like us, nowadays?

Stella   Like us? . . . I don't even know who you are, mister. 'Listen, officer, please. I just woke up, locked in an upstairs room with this man . . . disguised in a false moustache . . .'

Gordon (*under his breath, at 'man'*)   Bitch.

Stella 'Maybe he's just some kind of American spy, I dunno, sent here to poke and prod what's left of the country. I'd start by checking his papers.' Tell me, Gordon, who are they going to believe do you think, you or the girl who's been locked up?	**Gordon** (*to himself, from 'think'*) I shouldn't have stayed. I should have realised we'd end up here. Like this.

Pause.

I'm not the one holding the keys, here, Stella: the door's right over there. Anyway, my papers are just fine. I've got the hard-headed wife, the crazy kid crying herself to sleep every night back in Pennsylvania. I've got obligations to get back to. I've got every excuse to leave . . . No, it's you. It's you who should be the one who's worried, here.

Stella   Yes – of one big gangbang, right?

Gordon   Would you just . . . C'mon. Take seriously what I'm saying to you. For once. I'm trying desperately hard, now . . . I could. I could easily just . . .

Long pause.

Stella   Everybody does, Gordon.

She hides her face against her knees.

Gordon   Wait . . . Wait . . . No.

He steps over to her, his coat off, his shirt in disarray (buttoned badly) and with one of his own shoes now missing.

Gordon (*kneeling down in front of her*)   We'll go. Together. I can probably sneak us out and everything will be fine. There's your place, and there's Gary Hobsbaum's. Whichever comes first. We can make do. Pool our resources. We can make a run for it. All right?

Stella *looks up at him, passive now. She stares at his face. She turns to the bust, then back to* **Gordon**, *as if checking the resemblance. She lifts her hand and he rears back, for just a moment, afraid. Carefully, she takes her thumb and moves it across the place where the moustache was.*

Stella (*quietly*)   You're all red.

Gordon (*quietly*)   I am?

Stella (*quietly*)   And you're still so oblivious.

Gordon (*quietly*)   Fine. Okay.

Stella (*quietly*)   But . . .

Gordon   But what? What's-a-matter?

Stella   I don't . . . There's this awful feeling I have that none of this is happening the way it's supposed to and I'm not really here. I feel, so much, like I'm made of glass. Barely there, about to break.

Gordon   I know it. I know the feeling well.

Stella   God, I'm such a bloody mess.

Gordon   Me too. Look at me: I'm in pieces, here, already. Look, I'm the oblivious good-for-nothing hack. So let's just . . . Even if it's . . . We can at least try, Stella . . .

As she speaks, **Stella** *covers his mouth with the palm of her hand, then moves it, stroking his face.*

Stella   No. Please . . . I don't want to go back out there. You don't really know what . . . I've . . .

As **Gordon** *wraps his arms around her legs,* **Stella** *looks up to the skylight.*

Then a thud emanates from the closet.

Stella *and* **Gordon** *both jump back,* **Stella** *away from* **Gordon**.

The light flickers on in the closet.

Iris (*off stage*)   Shit.

Gordon *makes a move towards the door and waves for* **Stella** *to follow him.*

As **Iris** *peaks out from behind the curtain,* **Stella** *is the only one looking.*

Stella (*averting her eyes*)   No.

Gordon *rattles the doorknob.*

He moves back to **Stella** *again, sizing up the light behind the closet curtain.*

Gordon (*announcing to the wardrobe*)   Okay. Whoever's in there better come the hell out.

Stella (*from 'there'*)   No. Don't.

The light goes off in the closet.

Gordon *grabs* **Stella** *by the wrist.*

Gordon (*to* **Stella**)   It's okay. It's okay. (*To the closet.*) Now. Show yourself. There's really no point hiding if we know you're in there.

Iris *steps out, her hands held in surrender. She's holding the torch in one hand and a ring of keys in the other.*

Gordon   Now what's the idea? And, hang on, how'd you . . . if the door's already?

Stella (*looking at* **Iris***, from 'you'*)   She locked it, Gordon. She locked us in.

Gordon *steps towards* **Iris** *and, as soon as he does, she shines her torch directly in his face. He freezes.* **Iris** *then shines the light at* **Stella***.*

Stella *averts her gaze, as* **Iris** *makes a run for the couch. She jumps and sits down on the cushions, an animal scrunching herself up protectively, knees to her chest. Nervously, she pats her cheeks with her fingertips.*

Iris (*flicking her torch on and off*)   Look. I'm. Sorry. Sorry, sorry . . . Truly. I didn't mean it. I mean, I did. I just didn't want it to be all . . . like this.

Stella *twists her arm out of* **Gordon***'s grasp.*

I'm not so good at hiding. It's pretty funny. I keep getting these awful shakes. Marianne with the shaky hands, when I'm nervous. And it made me drop my torch, it did, my nervous system. Ha.

Gordon   What? Who are you?

He points accusatively, then reaches for **Stella**'s *wrist again.*

What do you think . . . ? (*To* **Stella**.) *Stella*, please let's –

Stella *turns completely away from the scene and rushes to the edge of the stage. She and* **Gordon** *now stand apart, with* **Stella** *farthest from the closet.*

Gordon (*to* **Iris**)   What d'you think you're doing?

Iris   You have no idea what's going on down there. You don't. It's all *crazy*. A real round up. Everyone's being taken away. Locked up. Teeth are being kicked out, bones broken. But what I don't get is that, if they end up taking everyone away, eventually, right, there's going to be no one left. They're going to have to surprise *themselves* in the night. I mean, this whole thing's crazy. It's gonna fall apart, has to, don't you think? It's like a bonkers game of hide and seek and soon everyone will be hiding from nothing . . . Just a lot of people standing there in the dark.

Gordon   What is she talking about? (*To* **Iris**.) You're gonna answer some questions right now, young lady. Or else. Stella, this is probably just the Manager's kid, I bet. Messing around. He mentioned something about his little spawn running amok. (*To* **Iris**.) I suppose you think this is some kinda joke? That you can just mess around with people like this?

Stella   Gordon, it's no use. She's here now.

Iris   My name is Iris. Okay? Now you know. I want to help. Now you know that too. It's why I'm here. I just want you to listen me now and maybe we can –

Gordon   Help? The whole Thames is ablaze, out there, missy, and you really think . . . ? Now you're going to put that pretty little flashlight down and hand over those keys. Right this minute. I don't care where you got them, but you're going to give them to me. Now.

Iris *stands up and holds out the keys but doesn't otherwise move.*

Gordon *steps towards her, and laughing she dodges him, faking to one side, playfully. They both freeze.*

Gordon   C'mon.

He tries again but, laughing even more now, **Iris** *manages to dodge him.*

Gordon (*lunging for her*)   You little bitch.

Iris *ducks away as he throws himself upon her, but he eventually manages to wrangle the keys out of her hands.*

Stella   You can't . . . Gordon. No.

Gordon (*struggling*)   Give me . . . Give it . . . To me, now.

Stella *hides her face in her hands.*

Gordon (*grasping the keys, victoriously*)   I'm gonna try every one of them, if I have to. (*He moves towards the door.*) We're getting out of here. Stella, get your shoes on.

He stands, facing the door. Then he slams the keys uselessly against the doorknob, kicking the door.

Pause. He feels desperately around the door frame, as if trying to get his fingers inside. Pushing.

Gordon   What've you done? Oh, Jesus.

Stella *lets her hands drop.*

Iris   It's locked. I know. We're locked in. Gordon, there was really nothing I could do . . . But look, it'll be okay. I can make it up to you. Right here, right now. I can make it up to you both . . . If you just let me.

Stella   And how do you intend on doing that?

Iris   Maybe, I can help you. To understand. We can help each other to –

Gordon   Understand what, exactly? There's nothing left to understand, here, honey. If we try breaking down that door, they're gonna come marching up here with their truncheons and their gags and all the rest of it. So, we're screwed.

Iris *laughs.*

We're screwed and you screwed us.

Iris *laughs again, more loudly, as she re-takes her place on the green couch.*

Gordon (*to himself*)   The skylight's too high . . . Even if we stacked these couches, one on top . . . (*He moves towards* **Stella**.) No, this is a sinking ship, now . . .

Stella   Stay the hell away from me. Don't you even dare come near me.

Gordon   What?

Stella   Did that excite you? Was it a turn on? I bet it was, wasn't it, this little performance just now? Have you got yourself hard again, doing that to a little girl? I bet you have, you sick . . . (*To* **Iris**.) Stay away from this creep, dear. This sick . . . *animal*.

Iris   I can look after myself thank you very much. I let him have them. They're no good to me anyway, those keys.

Gordon   All right, band together. I understand just fine. Persecute the only penis in the room.

Iris   Why are we talking like this? It'll be fine. We're safe here together, aren't we? Let's make the most of it while there's still time. I'm not just a kid, you know. Some helpless freak. You can learn things from me if only you both listened. I've got experience. With just this sort of thing . . . I'm not some grotty little hotel manager's daughter, either . . . I know that bitch and she's useless . . . I've *seen* things. (*She notices the projector.*) Hey, you've got a slide projector set up, already? That's *perfect*.

Gordon   There's nothing on that. Keep away.

Stella   There aren't any slides.

Iris   Well, let's talk then, why don't we? Not like this, but not like regular boring old everyday talk either. Not small talk. God, I hate that . . . I don't do small talk anymore, only real . . . conversations. With rude words and passion and secrets. Big ideas. Can't we try? While we wait, I mean.

Gordon (*to himself*)   'While we wait.' Jesus. Leave me out of this.

He shrugs and goes to the coffee table where he proceeds to take a thermos out and pour himself a cup.

Iris   Gordon. Trust me. They only want your money. And maybe your soul too, just for kicks. They're not about to save you, you realise. They're not doing anything you can't do yourself. They're sending you off with those, those false papers and that silly disguise because they want to get rid of you, so they can hand you over and forget you even existed . . . *Cunts*. Sometimes, you know, you should know this, they just collect your money, your life basically, and they leave you locked up in here, starving to death. Rooms full of starved forgotten people, Gordon. This hotel's full of them. It's all a bloody scam. It's not the way . . . And I think you know it's not . . .

Gordon *says nothing. Throughout* **Stella** *and* **Iris**'s *conversation he leafs through the book he found earlier.*

Stella   So, Iris?

She sits down slowly on the green couch, beside the girl.

Stella   Iris?

Iris   Hmm? Are we ready to talk now? I mean, can we really?

Stella   Yes, I think so . . . You and I can, anyway.

Iris   Good.

Long pause.

Iris   Well, ask a me question why don't you?

Stella   Okay . . . Where are you from? If you're not from here, I mean, if you're not from this place? You're aren't part of this, this *underground*, are you?

Iris   Underground?

Stella *turns to* **Gordon** *to see if he's heard this, but he doesn't react.*

Stella   One of those out to upset the system.

Iris   First, you should probably know that there is no underground. No such thing. Not really. There's only me as far as I can tell. And what I do, well, it isn't very underground at all. You know what I mean? It's up here. You're looking at it. Read 'em and weep. You can see me, can't you?

Stella   I can.

Iris   I'm right here, aren't I?

Stella   Yes, well –

Iris   Sitting beside you, right? Saying what I'm saying, wearing what I'm wearing. You hear my voice, you sense me next to you. My, I dunno, warmth or presence or whatever you want to call it. You see this upstairs room too, these lights. You perceive these things not only with your eyes, but with your whole entire body. Head, shoulders, knees, toes. So . . . this is where it happens, out here in the open. I'm here because you see me. And you're here because I see you. My body, your body. My brain, your mind. It's all just a matter of paying attention or not paying attention. *Believing.* You have to decide. Commit. Be present. Get ready for revelations and stuff.

Stella   I see. But you still haven't quite answered –

Iris   Where I'm from?

Stella   Yes.

Iris   Oh, here, there. Out in the wilderness, these days . . . Abandoned by my mother and father, I took to the wilds.

Gordon (*chuckling*)   Oh brother. We're not buying it, kiddo.

Iris   It's the truth. I swear. I've been staying out on the Heath, now, for weeks. Out in the open air, living and sleeping with the trees. And do you know what I saw, just – when was it – *yesterday*? Yesterday, while I was out there, lying beside an old tree? Can you guess? The sun came up more golden than I can ever remember seeing it before. And there was a sort of burning in all the leaves. An inner light, maybe, to match the outer one. A radiance in this lovely old tree. And, as I noticed this, I saw that there were birds. There in branches. That the birds were coming back. Yes. Tiny sparrows all puffed up. So small and fragile and yet so, so, so . . . alive. Huddled up together against this brilliant sky . . . It looked like heaven to me.

Gordon   Hell of a heaven . . . You do know that this sky you say looks so goddamn pretty is falling in, right now. As we speak.

Iris   Even so . . .

Gordon   Well, there's no point pretending.

Stella (*to* **Gordon**)   I thought you'd chosen not to speak, Gordon. I thought you were leaving yourself out of this.

Iris   But it's not going to work unless we all –

Stella   Please go on, Iris. I want to hear more . . .

Gordon   Listen to this instead. 'The existence,' it says here. 'The existence of other people is a difficulty and an outrage.' How d'you like them (*Bad French.*) *sentiments*?

Iris (*to* **Gordon**)   But it's a surprise too, isn't it? Really. At the end of the day –

Stella   Pay no attention to him.

Iris (*to* **Gordon**)   It's like, I surprise you and you surprise me.

Stella   Continue. Iris. Please, go on.

Iris   Well, okay . . . okay. Yeah: it's like this story I know.
I'm not sure where from. I thought of it the other day and it
made me laugh. I was hysterical, right there in the middle of
the street remembering it . . . 'There was once an owl.'
Okay? This little owl, barely brave enough to fly. And she
was, though this I know is gonna sound very odd for an owl,
she was totally afraid of the dark. Right. Every night, this
little owl flies down to a little pond in middle of the forest,
and because she's so afraid of the dark, she stares down at
her reflection. Pretending, you know. That it's somebody
else there keeping her company in the dark. Night after
night it happens like this. 'Hello, Miss Owl,' she says. 'Hello,
Miss Owl,' the reflection answers back. And the darkness
doesn't feel so fucking scary anymore . . . But then, this one
night, something very funny happens.

Stella (*to herself*)   I think I know this from somewhere. How
do I . . . ?

Iris *switches the torch on.*

Iris (*suddenly very serious, quiet*)   The owl flies down again to
the little pond, and just as she's about to say good evening to
herself for about the thousandth, the thousandth scary
night, she sees (**Iris**, *here, switches on her torch*) this big golden
fish, swimming there beneath her. She says, 'Hello, Mr Fish,'
and he says back to her, 'Hello, Miss Owl.' I mean, wow,
right? He asks her what she is doing there and she explains.
She tells him how afraid she's been. Then he says, 'Well,
that's absolutely the strangest thing . . . For the longest time,
I've been down here afraid of the water. So afraid, in fact,
that I've been coming to this side of the pond every night,
just so I can look up at the moonlight and listen to your
voice. Just so I could feel I had some company here in this
lonely pond.'

Stella (*quietly*)   Oh my God. I feel dizzy.

Iris *switches off the torch.*

Gordon (*yawning*)   You're not the only one. It's all a trick, Stella. I'm not listening to a word of it.

Stella   Where did you say you first heard this story?

Iris (*shrugging*)   It's just something that occurred to me one day, out of the blue. I thought it was funny –

Stella   Out of the blue? . . . Iris, this is *my* story, you realise. This is a story I used to tell myself. When I was . . . Well, I made it up a very long time ago.

Gordon   Oh please. It's Hans Christian Andersen, or I don't know, somebody else annoyingly Scandinavian. I've heard it too.

Stella   No, I remember this. Gordon, I told you about the rock pool. This is one of the stories from the upstairs room . . . This really happened. The fish, the pond. I was that little girl. This was my life. No, I'm the one who thought of that owl who was afraid of the dark.

Gordon (*standing up*)   I need some air. Anyone care to join me?

Iris (*excited*)   A walk? Where?

But **Gordon** *is already moving to the back of the room, waving her off.*

Gordon   The real world, I think.

Iris   Oh.

Stella   Iris, Iris. Now you must tell me. You must remember where you heard that story.

Iris *looks up at her and the two women stare into each other's eyes, sharing something intense.*

Gordon, *fed up, has begun fiddling with the radio.*

Stella *strokes* **Iris**'s *hand. Then she squeezes it tight. They stare at one another, sharing something intense.*

Iris   You're turning red, you know.

Stella *looks down at* **Iris***'s wrist, embarrassed.*

Long pause.

Stella   These marks on your arm? Iris?

Iris *pulls down her sleeve.*

Iris (*secretively*)   Maybe it would help, if you told him what you were going to, Stella.

Stella   Tell him?

Iris   What you were about to. Earlier, just before I got all shaky and messed things up behind the curtain.

Stella   I really have no idea what you're –

Gordon   Stella. She's a lunatic. We've been locked in a room with a schizophrenic.

Pause.

Iris (*secretive*)   No. About the roof, I mean. About being late. About being afraid. Before.

Stella   Late? . . . No. I don't . . .

Gordon   This is perfect. A flashlight toting proto-terrorist. Really, I should be writing this down. Has anyone seen my typewriter? . . . Oh right, I still need to find that paper.

Iris   Why don't you just –

Stella (*scolding*)   Iris, no. Shhh.

Iris   But you *want* to. So tell him. I think it would help. You can make him understand. Go on. It'll be okay.

Gordon   Well, I'm on tenterhooks now. By 'him', I assume you're talking about me? Because I'm not sure I want to be a party to this. Whatever you two sisters are cooking up over there.

Iris   Yes. Gordon. She was going to tell you, but then she didn't.

Gordon   Why do you keep calling me . . . Why'd you keep acting like you know who I am?

Iris (*to* **Stella**, *from 'acting'*)   Maybe you should just tell him. Yes. For real this time. Like you were going to. Before the shaking came all over me.

Stella   No, no. Iris.

Iris   You were up there on the roof, weren't you . . .

Stella (*whispering*)   No. That's not right. It wasn't –

Iris   The meeting place was all arranged. But you had, you got the time wrong. Everyone was already gone. And you were up there all alone, Stella, with no one left to . . . and that's when, that's when you knew you couldn't –

Stella *lunges at* **Iris**, *pressing a hand to her mouth.*

Gordon (*sitting up*)   Whoa, whoa.

Stella   Stop it. You shut up, you awful little . . .

Stella, *grabs one of the cushions on the couch and begins smothering* **Iris**.

Gordon, *meanwhile, leaps over the coffee table, rushing to* **Iris**'s *aid.*

Gordon   Hey.

Gordon *separates them both, grabbing* **Stella** *first. She pushes him away and he lands on top of* **Iris**.

Stella (*hurt, broken*)   There. There, you two. That's it. That's what you've really been wanting to do, isn't it? That's what this is all about, what's really going on behind the scenes . . .

Gordon (*jumping back, hands in surrender*)   Keep me out of it.
I came here, I thought, to get away from all this, these mind
games, accusations.

Iris, *curls up on the couch, hugging her knees, shaking, fidgeting,
her hands covering her ears.*

Stella   Oh God, I'm going to be sick. You two are a perfect
team, a perfect little romance. Really. I can't take this. I can't.
Not anymore. (*To the skylight.*) Just get it over with already.
Just leave me alone.

Gordon *glares at* **Stella** *for a moment, then rushes for the intercom.
He picks up the phone and begins buzzing down repeatedly.*

Gordon (*screaming*)   All right, if that's it, then come and get
us, you sons-a-bitches. We're all up here. I'm sure you can
find it. Come put us all out of our misery now or we're
gonna do it for you. Let's go: what's taking you so damned
long? We're up here and we aren't going anywhere.

He slams the phone back down again.

Gordon   It's over, now. It's all over. So now we wait. (*To*
Stella.) Sit. (*To* **Iris**.) Sit. No one has to talk to anybody.
Nobody has to tell anyone anything. It's done, finito. All
right? I'm finished. We're all fucking finished.

He grabs his coat off the floor and puts it on.

Stella (*arms folded*)   What are you doing?

Gordon *sits down on the red couch again, and begins pouring out
two more cups of coffee from the thermos.*

Gordon   I'm sorry, it's cooled off, but that's all there is.

The lights flicker.

Absentees. It's a fitting word for what we are, don't you
think? Stella? *Absentees.*

Pause.

Iris *jumps up, overturning the coffee table, spilling the drinks. She stomps back to closet, hiding inside and pulling back the curtain.*

Gordon *picks up one of the cups from the floor and drinks what's left inside it.*

Nowhere else to go, I guess.

Pause. **Stella** *goes to the green couch and slumps down in* **Iris***'s place.*

Stella (*laughing*)   She's probably, in there, thinking of ways to top herself. But it'll be, it'll all be useless. God. Nothing to slit her wrists with. No pills . . . No, I'll tell you what, I suppose, I suppose, she could use the batteries from that torch . . . Can you imagine that? The acid eating away at you from the inside. Poor girl.

Gordon   Go to hell, Stella. Would you, please? Just go to hell.

Stella (*from laughing hysterically to crying*)   Yes, perhaps she might just as well eat the contents of that little lavatory. She does look a little anorexic, after all. The curtains, the taps. Down in one . . . The poor girl . . . She could probably use the, um . . .

Static from the radio, interrupting. A station is coming through. Voices: **Stella** *and* **Gordon***'s, through the static, talking happily, cheerfully.*

Gordon *and* **Stella***, sitting on the couch, listen attentively to themselves.*

Gordon (*from the radio*)   And that one time. In the trees.

Stella (*radio*)   Yes. The sun in our eyes. I could barely see it was so bright.

Gordon   What? D'you hear that?

Gordon (*radio*)   I remember all those birds. Singing everywhere. Around us.

Stella (*weeping slightly*)   Wait. Listen.

Gordon (*radio*)   The heat, and your face looking up at me like that. Yes, I remember.

Stella (*radio*)   Making love in that meadow, with you, down along the riverbank . . .

Gordon (*radio*)   In a way, it seems so brave, now. Looking back. The way we used to just, do that. Out in the open.

Stella (*radio*)   With the sun in your eyes, you leaned into me.

Stella (*from the couch*)   I remember this. I remember hearing this too, but . . . ?

Gordon (*radio*)   Both of us, like that. I could barely see you either. The long grass all around . . .

Stella (*radio*)   And the wind. And the trees blowing and the little bridge.

Gordon (*radio*)   Yes . . . You and I . . . Beside the bridge, beforehand . . . You broke a wineglass and you said it would bring us good luck.

The voices fade, through the static.

Gordon   At the bridge. At the bridge? No. But I would have . . .

The lamplights flicker out.

Gordon   This is crazy. I don't want this. I don't have to listen. I can't.

Stella (*calmly*)   Gordon.

*The light from behind the curtain, meanwhile, is bright with the glow from **Iris**'s torch.*

Iris *steps very slowly but dramatically out. She is wearing **Gordon**'s moustache. She wields her torch like a microphone, but doesn't bring it to her face until she's come centre stage and hit her mark.*

Iris   Good evening.

Gordon   What are you doing? Why are you playing these games, huh? You can't just go playing games with people . . . With people's lives.

Iris   This isn't a game I'm playing. I'm being absolutely serious now, so that you can finally see what I'm trying to show you. Look . . . Now really look at me.

Long pause.

I'm playing you right now, Gordon. In a devastating performance, really really heartbreaking, so try and pay attention. (*American accent.*) 'My name is Gordon and I came here to get away from everything. At least I thought I was. I thought I could put an end to everything, watch it all sink around me and maybe sink along with it. But it's still right in front of my face, only I don't want to look. So I just keep turning away, holing up in various rooms, leaving them again . . . and again . . . and again.'

She hits the projector, which instantly begins running the two motion sequences seen earlier, looped over and over again.

'Look . . . These images from another time and place, too blackened, too covered in ash to remember properly now. Before everything. Before all of this. It hurts. It stings. I know.'

Gordon (*stumbling towards* **Iris**)   Stop. Stop it. Now. I don't want you to . . . Don't go any further.

Iris (*backing away*)   I have to Gordon. No, no, I have to, I have to if you won't. The bridge, the light, that time you both –

Gordon (*standing in the projector light*)   Dreams. Lies. Imaginary things. All of it. No. You can't do this . . .

Iris (*American*)   'I, Gordon, was standing here alone in the dark of this room, left alone here and looking up at this skylight, and I found myself . . . I found myself praying.

Praying to I-don't-know-what, but praying. Praying, God, that these things, at least, that these things might stay. That these things won't just sink away with all the rest. (*Pause.*) I have to imagine them. I really must: a time before all this . . .'

The projector flickers to a halt. Darkness, now, except for the empty projector light on **Gordon**.

Scene Five

Gordon (*deflating, understanding*)   I think I can. Maybe, I can, now. Handle it. I want to . . . do this.

Stella   Are you sure, Gordon? This is, really, what you want?

The slide changes and **Stella** *gives a little gasp. It shows* **Gordon**, *fresh-faced and sitting at a desk, in front of a typewriter.* **Gordon** *stands to one side, very near the projection, as if giving a presentation.*

Gordon   Yes. This here . . . This is a writer who can't write. Who still can't get out of his own way. The schmuck. Look at him. He exiles himself in the room upstairs every morning and the stories disappear beneath him. It's an escape he chases, daily, but never quite manages. He actually arranges for a telephone to be installed in this room, one which only makes outgoing calls. No one to get a hold of him unless he calls them first. That was the system. God, this is pitiful.

A picture of a woman's hands over **Gordon**'s *eyes.*

Gordon   I don't know what this is. No.

A picture of the bust resting on a cluttered mantle, in a different house.

Ah. This is my good friend Gary Hobsbaum.

An old pornographic slide, a woman alone, legs spread.

Gordon (*quickly*)   No.

*A picture of **Stella**. One of the stills from the earlier bedroom scene.*

I really can't . . . No, I'm not sure where this comes in the chronology. Where it fits. Before or after.

Iris *directs the torchlight at **Gordon**'s face.*

Iris   It doesn't matter, Gordon. Go on. Continue. *Think it out . . .*

Gordon   Ah. (*A little choked up, suddenly.*) Um . . . She's . . . Her name. Her name is Stella.

Pause.

Stella . . . We met, a very long time ago, at a dinner party. And, when I told her that I was a writer . . . This was always the first thing that I told anyone, even though I hadn't written a thing yet, hadn't amounted to anything, even then . . . I was dreaming . . . And when I told her this dream of mine, told this woman, she responded . . . Revealing to me an amazing story of her own. It was a secret she kept as a little girl, of writing stories to herself in an old attic room. In this grand old house. Writing as if she were sending letters, folded up secrets. Messages in a bottle. It was the most beautiful thing . . . And I felt. God, and I just felt . . . I wanted so much to protect her then . . . Stella. As she was. As we were, her and I. *Guiltless*. For a time. Together. Sans regret.

He crumbles up, not saying anymore. Long pause.

Stella (*standing*)   Go back. Go back again, Iris. If we can? I want to see him again, as *he* was before too. I'm sorry Gordon, but I can't resist. It'll help me remember too.

*Back to the image of **Gordon** working at his desk. **Stella** give a little gasp of appreciation before she begins.*

Ah . . . Yes, now, we met at a dinner party. And he . . . he reminded me vaguely of this boy I used to play with as a girl.

A boy named Dragan who lived next door. Also of my father, vaguely . . . Something about him . . . But enough for there to be this shock of recognition. Then he told me that he was a writer, and about all the books he wanted to write, and it was like a window into his soul or his future, in a sense . . . And so I told him, yes, the whole story of my childhood, hiding away in the upstairs room of my childhood home, and all those tales I used to collect for imaginary people . . . And it was then, only then . . . After I'd met Gordon for the first time, the man who would soon become my husband, it was then that I remembered one of them. One of the old stories I'd written. I thought I'd forgotten them all, that all of them had gone up in smoke, but this one, it returned to me out of the blue, talking with Gordon, this little folktale about an owl who goes down to a pond every night and meets a fish there. It was inspired by something that had happened to me. You see, I was in the habit of sneaking out my bedroom window. On clear, quiet nights, I used to go down to make wishes at the rock pool. And I found, one evening, while everyone else was asleep, and the ivy and the gravel drive they were all so blue and quiet . . .

Iris *directs the torchlight at her face.*

I found this coy fish swimming around in there, in the water. Right beneath me, surfacing from below . . . Like something out of a dream. But really, absolutely, definitively, there. Very soft and slow. Very orange and lithe. Logically, one of my parents must have bought it and placed it there without telling me. But I never found out, and I never wanted to, really . . . To me it had to remain this magical, secret thing . . . And here I was suddenly, revealing it, disclosing what seemed to me a deep miraculous secret inside myself. Spilling myself out, inexplicably, for this tall mustachioed American I'd run into at a dinner party.

Iris *switches off the torch.*

The slides flick ahead again, to an image of **Stella** *holding a camera to her eye.*

Gordon   Later, when she started taking pictures, she told me I had an American face. It showed up particularly well in black and white, according to her . . . Like Robert Redford's, she said . . . All these pictures she took, all these lost moments . . . It was her father's camera, an old Olympus she dug out of the basement one day for no particular reason . . . Then pictures, pictures, all the time. Like she was wrangling with something, trying to prove a point, this whole new energy coming over her. And, to tell the truth, it frightened me a little. Made me wary of her. Also, pretty jealous.

Iris *switches off the torch.*

Because she was producing the work, mountains of work, and, I mean, there I was toiling in my little room, trying to *think* my way out of oblivion . . . Her instincts astounded me, that she could be so intuitive, so natural and off-the-cuff. Anyway, I burned all her pictures. In the end. Afterwards. Piles and piles of them. On a makeshift bonfire in the backyard . . . I burned them all before I left . . . for England.

The slide changes. Showing **Gordon** *alone in the upstairs room, looking up at the skylight.*

Iris   And why did you come? . . . Gordon? How did you end up here?

Gordon   It had to be.

Iris *again directs the torchlight at his face.*

It had to be here, because this was where . . . she came from. And this was the only place I could think of coming . . . to look for her. Here. Where everything was ending. Her story, her point of origin. It was disappearing, it was sinking, so I had to come. Before it was too late. The place where she started – I wanted to find it in the darkness. One last flicker of light, one last time.

The slide changes. An image of **Gordon**'s *face from the first sequence. His face against* **Stella**'s *neck.*

Iris *turns off the torch.*

Stella *reappears in the projector light.*

Stella   *Time* . . . .Time went on and she would keep going up to the roof at night. Trying she told him, to get her thoughts together. To sort things out. Things she couldn't tell him, and things he was always too afraid to ask her about. The little scars that marked her wrist. The crying in her sleep . . . He never guessed she might be trying. Trying to work up the nerve . . . In the days and months that followed, he would wonder to himself how he could leave her so alone. Why he hadn't just gone upstairs and held her hand. Taken hold of her, before she took . . . herself . . .

The projection goes black. Darkness.

Gordon *now stands under the skylight.*

Gordon   Oh God. Oh God. I don't know that I can do this, Iris. I can't go any further. No. Oh God. All this leaving, I can't take any more. I want to stay. Here. It's too much, otherwise. Don't let this happen. Don't leave me behind. Please, please, God, don't leave me behind, here, in this place. Please don't leave me.

The lamplight slowly rises.

The room as it was before, only **Stella** *is gone. Daylight from above.* **Gordon** *stands there with the torch for a moment, while* **Iris** *waits on the red couch.*

Gordon   Stella?

Iris   She's gone, Gordon. She's not here anymore. Remember?

Gordon *nods, understanding.*

Gordon   Oh. Yes.

He sets the torch down on the coffee table. He sits opposite **Iris**.

Gordon   Is it . . . is it almost time? Do you have to go now too? You don't . . . ?

Iris   No, no. I can stay.

Gordon   You don't have to go, yet? There's still time left?

Iris   Really, we don't have to keep worrying about the time, Gordon . . . Let's just sit here together. Okay? . . . For a little while.

Gordon   Okay. (*Pause.*) Thank you, Iris . . . Thank you for coming.

Fade to black.

For a complete catalogue
of Methuen Drama titles
write to:

Methuen Drama
Bloomsbury Publishing Plc
50 Bedford Square
London WC1B 3DP

or you can visit our website at:

www.methuendrama.com